ook belongs to

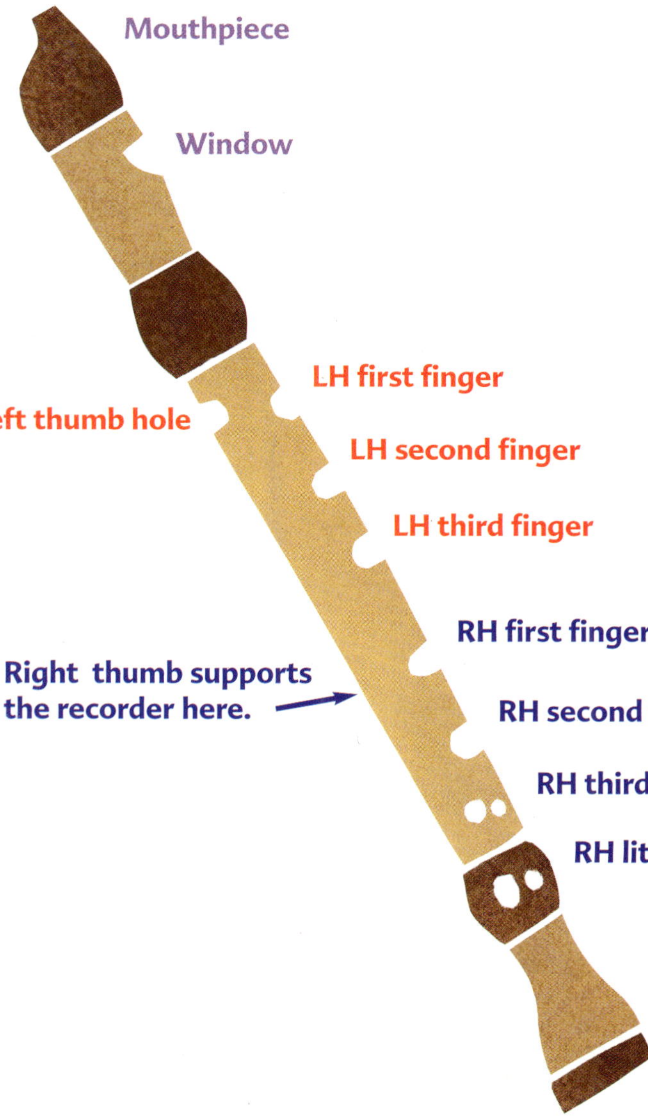

Left hand above,
Right hand below,
Nice straight back
And ready to blow.

Play along with a Recorder Magic CD. Visit www.recordermagic.co.uk to find out more.

THE A & C BLACK RECORDER SERIES

DESCANT TUTOR BOOK 1

Recorder Magic

Elliot Lewis

Jane Sebba & David Moses

Recorder Magic
Book 1

By David Moses and Jane Sebba

A & C Black • London

www.recordermagic.co.uk

Spooky Spinney

Walking late through Spooky Spinney
Gives me wobbly knees,
When I hear the wintery wind
Whispering through the trees.

Blow gently

Walking late through Spooky Spinney
Gives me wobbly knees,
When I hear the wintery wind
Moaning through the trees.

Blow a little harder

Sound effects

Support the recorder with your right thumb.
Cover the window of the recorder with the first finger of your left hand.

Whispering: blow very gently down your recorder.

Moaning and roaring: blow a little harder as the wind gets stronger.

Wailing: take your left finger away and blow.

**Perform this with a friend.
After your friend has read each verse, make the sound effect on your recorder.**

**Walking late through Spooky Spinney
Gives me wobbly knees,
When I hear the wintery wind
Roaring through the trees.**

Blow harder still

**Walking late through Spooky Spinney
Gives me wobbly knees,
When I hear the ghouls and ghosties
Wailing through the trees.**

Take your left finger away and blow

New note B

Make sure that your left thumb and first finger cover their holes completely.

Support the recorder with your right thumb.

Remember to sit up straight.

Choose an item on the menu and say it:

fish	in	a	fruit	cake

'Doo' the rhythm:

fish	in	a	fruit	cake
doooo	doo-doo		doooo	doooo

Play the rhythm on the note B:

fish	in	a	fruit	cake
B	B	B	B	B

Today's menu

Fish in a fruit cake
Ice-cream sandwiches
Sausage with whipped cream
Ants in chocolate
Eel pie and peanuts

Tonguing

Practise tonguing by saying the word 'doo'. Then place the tip of the mouthpiece between your lips and position your fingers for the note B.
Whisper 'doo' down the recorder.
Try a short 'doo'. Try a long 'dooooo'.

Today's Specials

B Stir	B fried	B B lol - li -	B pop.
B Lamb	B B chop and	B cus -	B tard.
B B Cher - ries	B and	B fish	B paste.
B Jam	B with	B bean	B B cur - ry.

Crotchet

A crotchet lasts for one beat.

Quavers

Each quaver lasts for half a beat.

pop	pop	pop	pop
lol-ly	lol-ly	lol-ly	lol-ly

- Say the words of each rhythm out loud.
- Clap each rhythm.
- Play each rhythm on the note B.

New note A

Don't blow;
just finger B.
To play A, cover
the next hole
down with your
second finger
and blow.

City rhythms

A Glas -	A A gow in	A Scot -	A land.
A Bom -	A A bay in	A A In - di -	A a.

Crotchet rest

Be silent for one beat.

Running round the world

A A Run - ning	A A round the	A world	A from	A east	A to	A west.	
A Out	A of	A breath?		A Take	A a	A rest.	

Barline and double barline

Music is divided into bars by barlines.

The double barline shows the end of the piece.

Duet

A duet is a piece for two players or two groups of players.

- In this duet, one player plays the red part and the other plays the blue part.
- In the final bar, both play at the same time to sound like a car horn.

Animals on the road (duet)

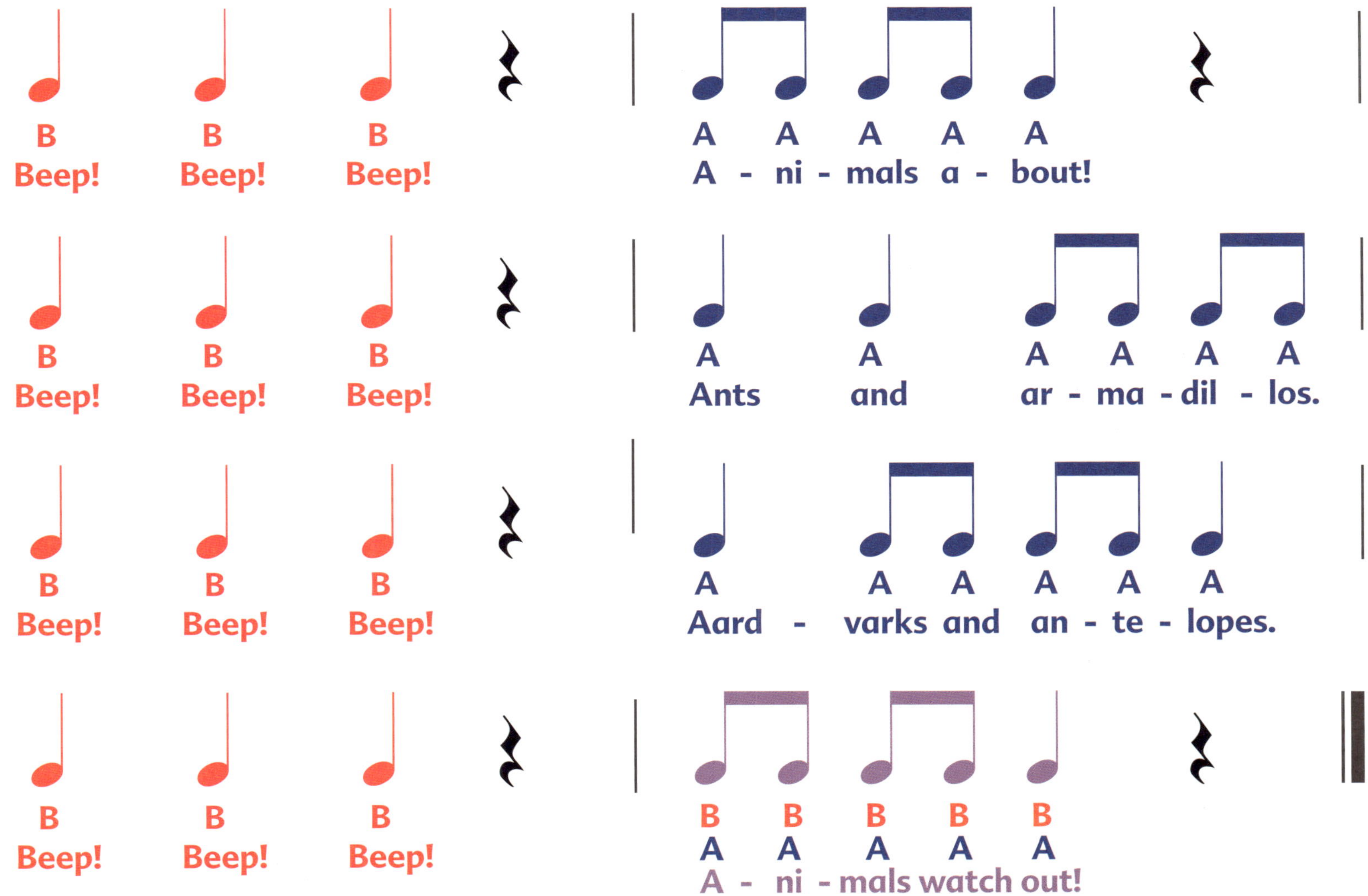

How to read B

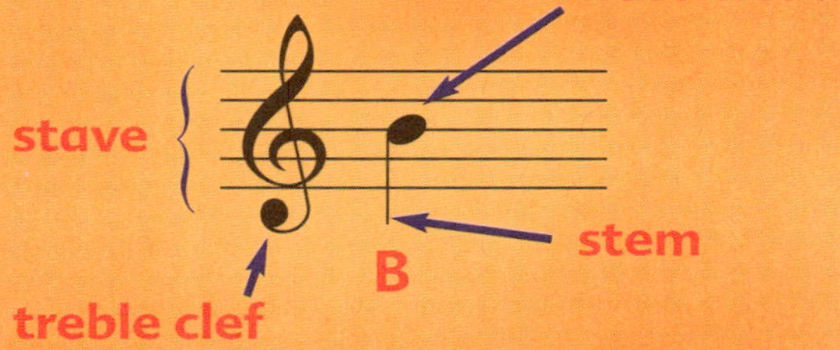

The note B sits on the middle line of the stave.

Clean clothes

How to read A

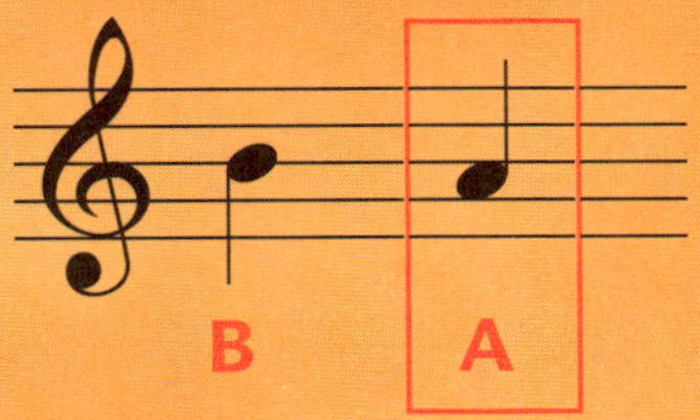

The note A sits in the space below the middle line.

Time signature

4 ← Four
4 ← crotchet beats in a bar.

A and B

Gymnastics

One recorder

Going to School

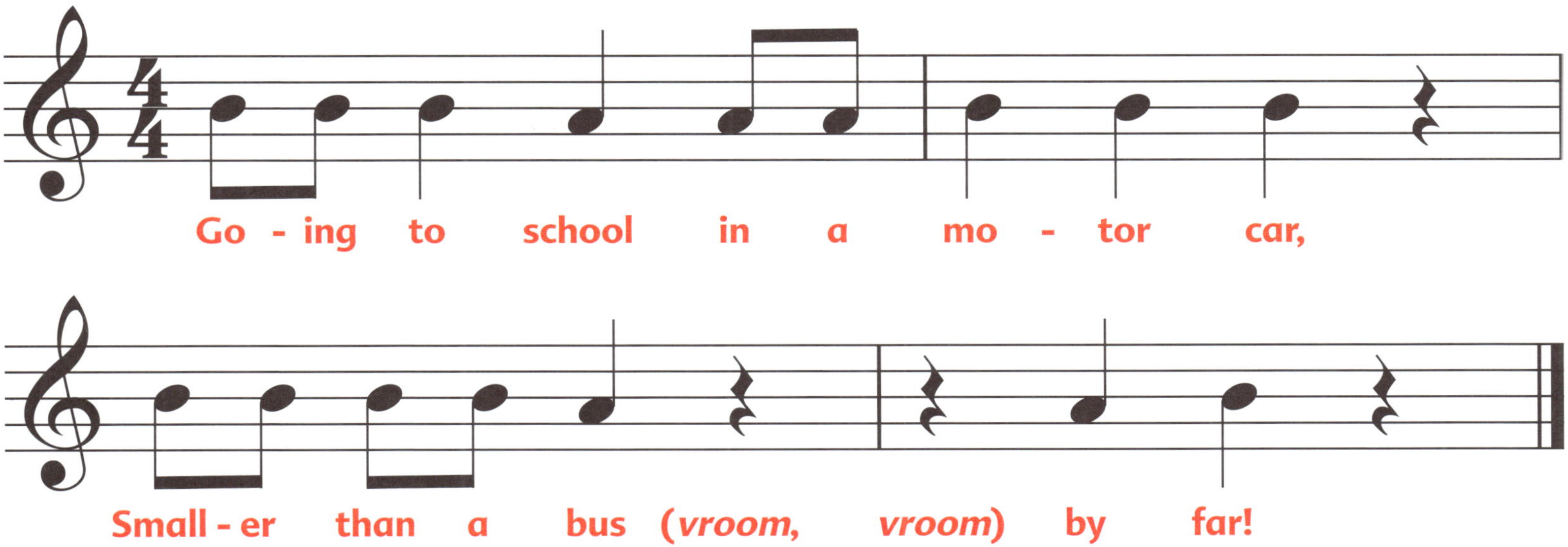

New note G

Position your left hand so that you can cover all four holes comfortably with your fingers and thumb.

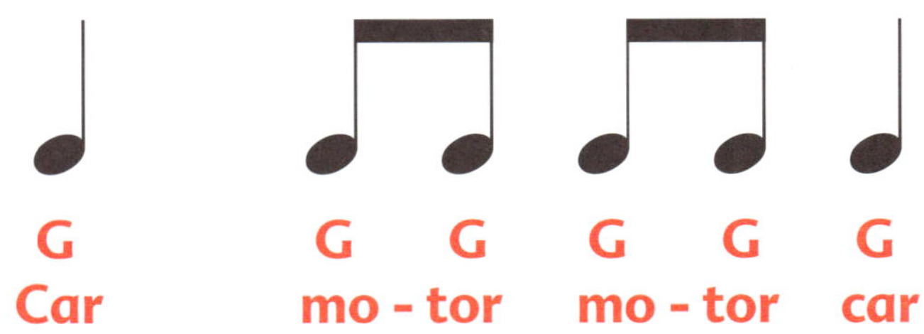

Ostinato

An ostinato is a pattern of notes repeated again and again.

- Play the motor car rhythm four times as an ostinato while someone else plays *Going to school.*
- Make sure that you both start at the same time and play at the same speed.

How to read G

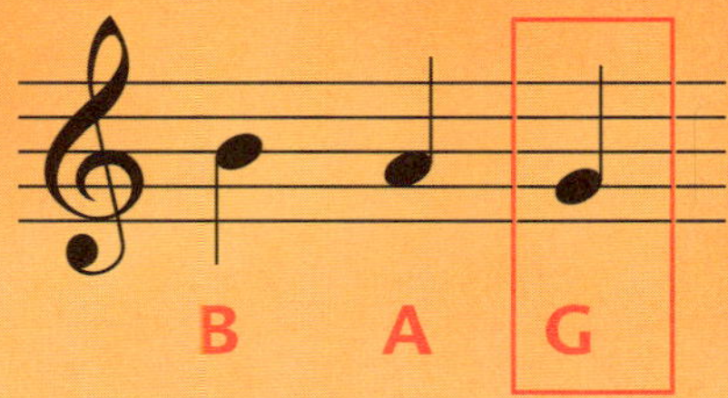

Minim

A minim lasts for two beats.

Breath-taking butterflies

But - ter - flies tak - ing breath, Breath - tak - ing but - ter - flies.

Swallow flying high

Swal - low fly - ing high, High - fly - ing swal - low.

Time flies (round)

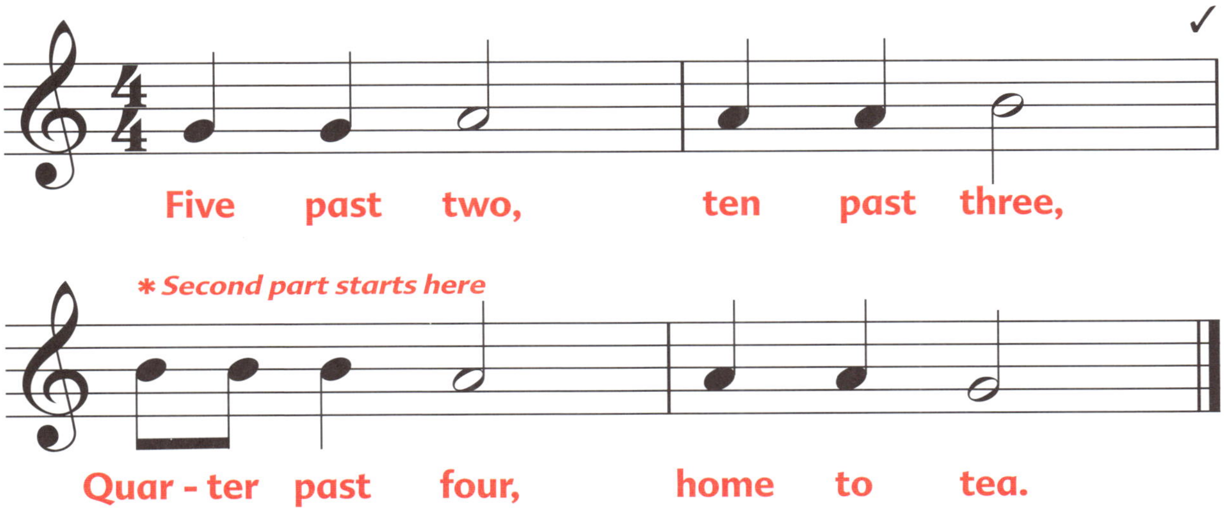

Green jelly

Breath mark

✓

Take a breath when you see this sign.

Round

A round is a piece of music for two or more players starting one after another. It can be played (or sung) over and over again.

Repeat sign

When you reach this sign, go back to the beginning and play the music again.

Rover

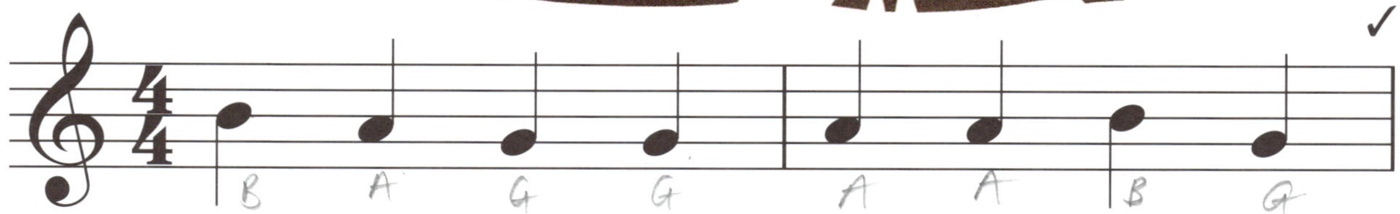

I've a dog, his name is Ro - ver,
When he's good, he's good all o - ver,

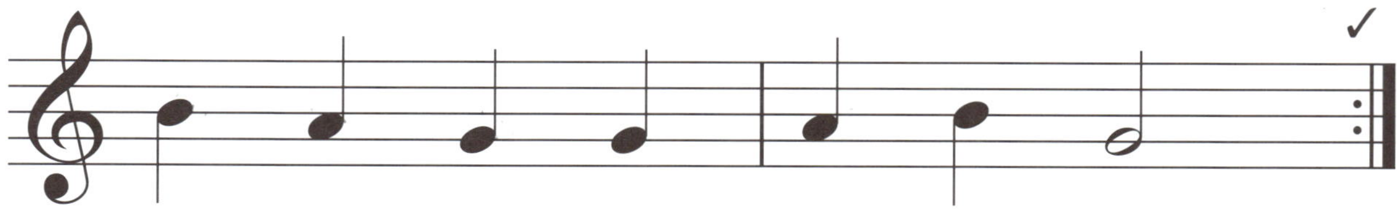

He's my dog and he's the best.
When he's bad he's just a pest.

Black and white cat

Black and white cat on a black and white rug,

Gent - ly pick it up and give it a hug.

Time signature

3/4 — Three crotchet beats in a bar.

Friends on holiday

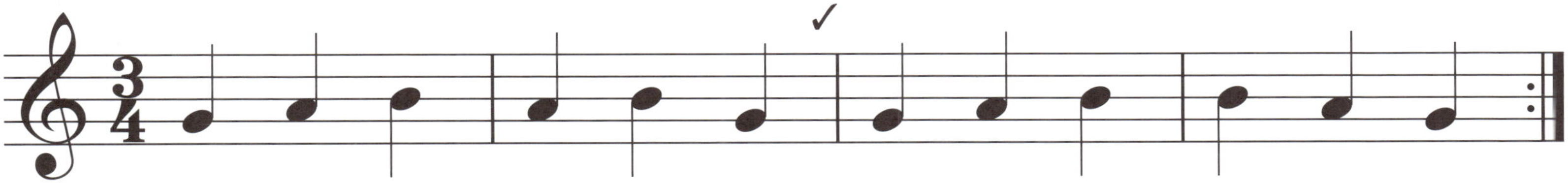

Little Bo Peep

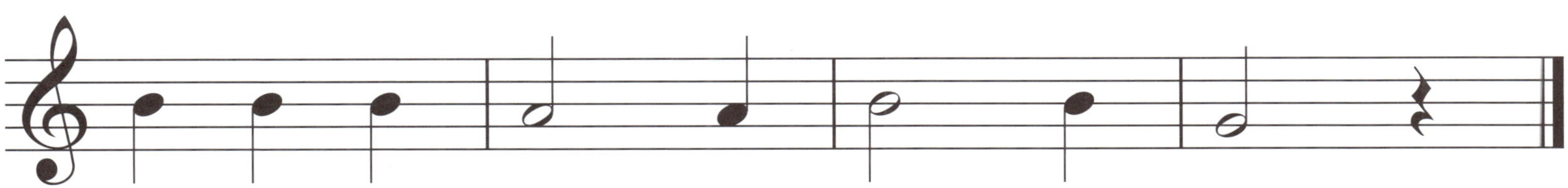

Dotted minim

A minim with a dot after it lasts for three beats.

Time for Sleep

Ducks' delight

Ask a friend to make a duck sound effect whenever they see the picture.

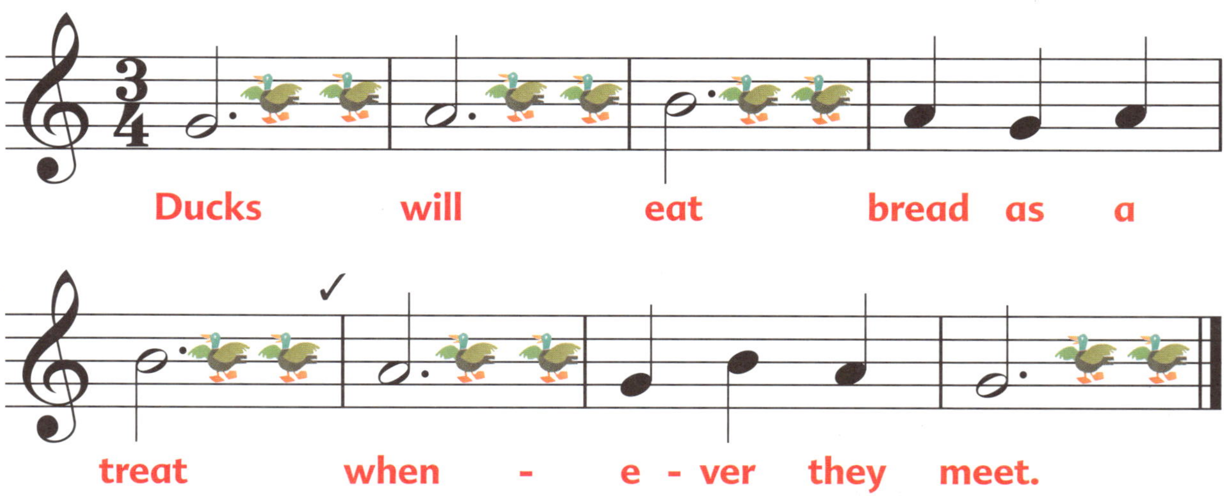

Terrapin Tim (duet)

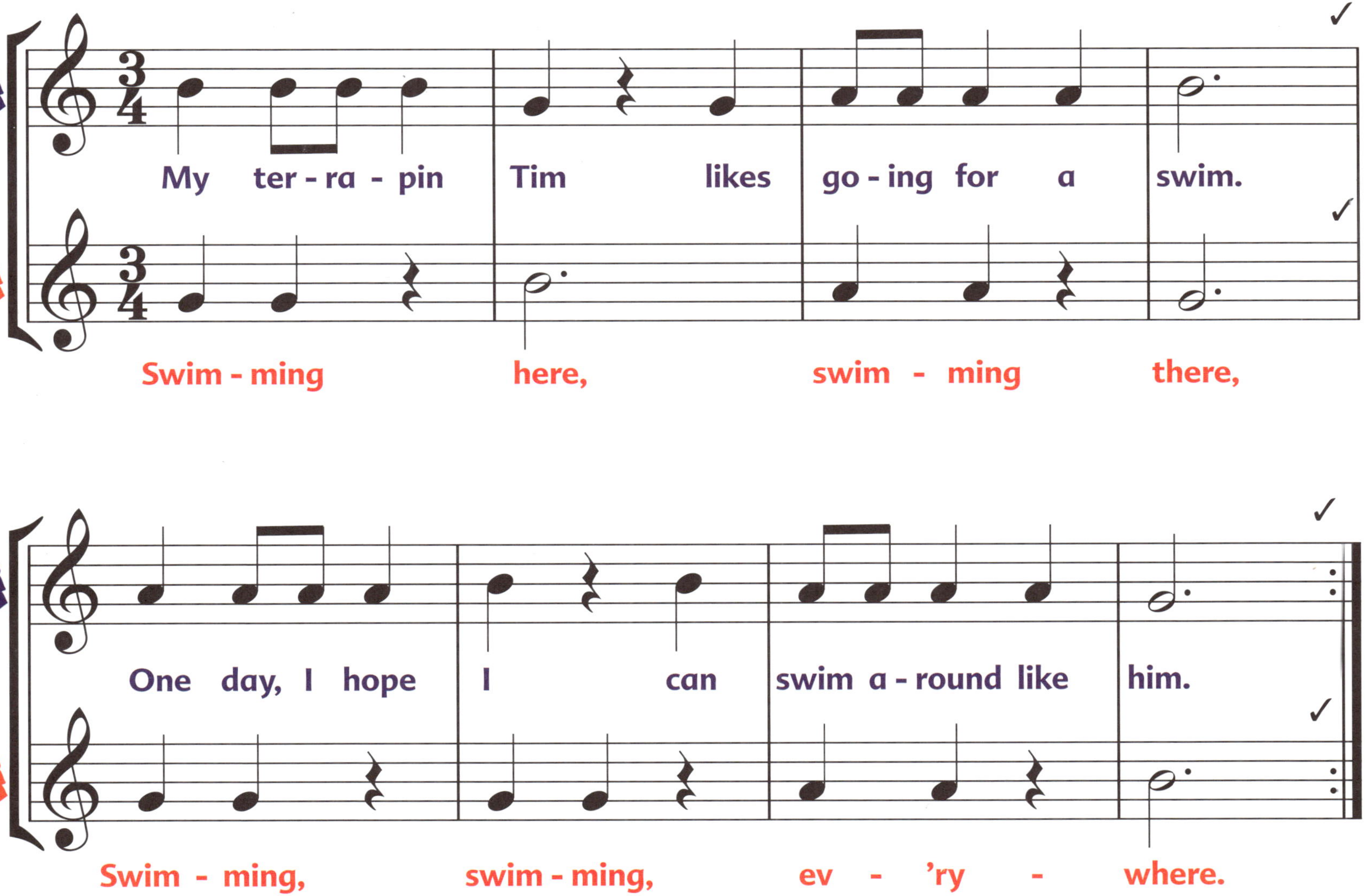

New note E

Don't blow - just finger G. To play E, add the first two fingers of your right hand.

- Decide who will play the red and who will play the blue part.
- Swap parts for the repeat.
- Then ignore the colours and play the piece all the way through.

Big kite (duet)

High heels and trainers

Time signature

2 ← Two
4 ← crotchet beats in a bar.

One mosquito

Cover the window of the recorder and blow hard.

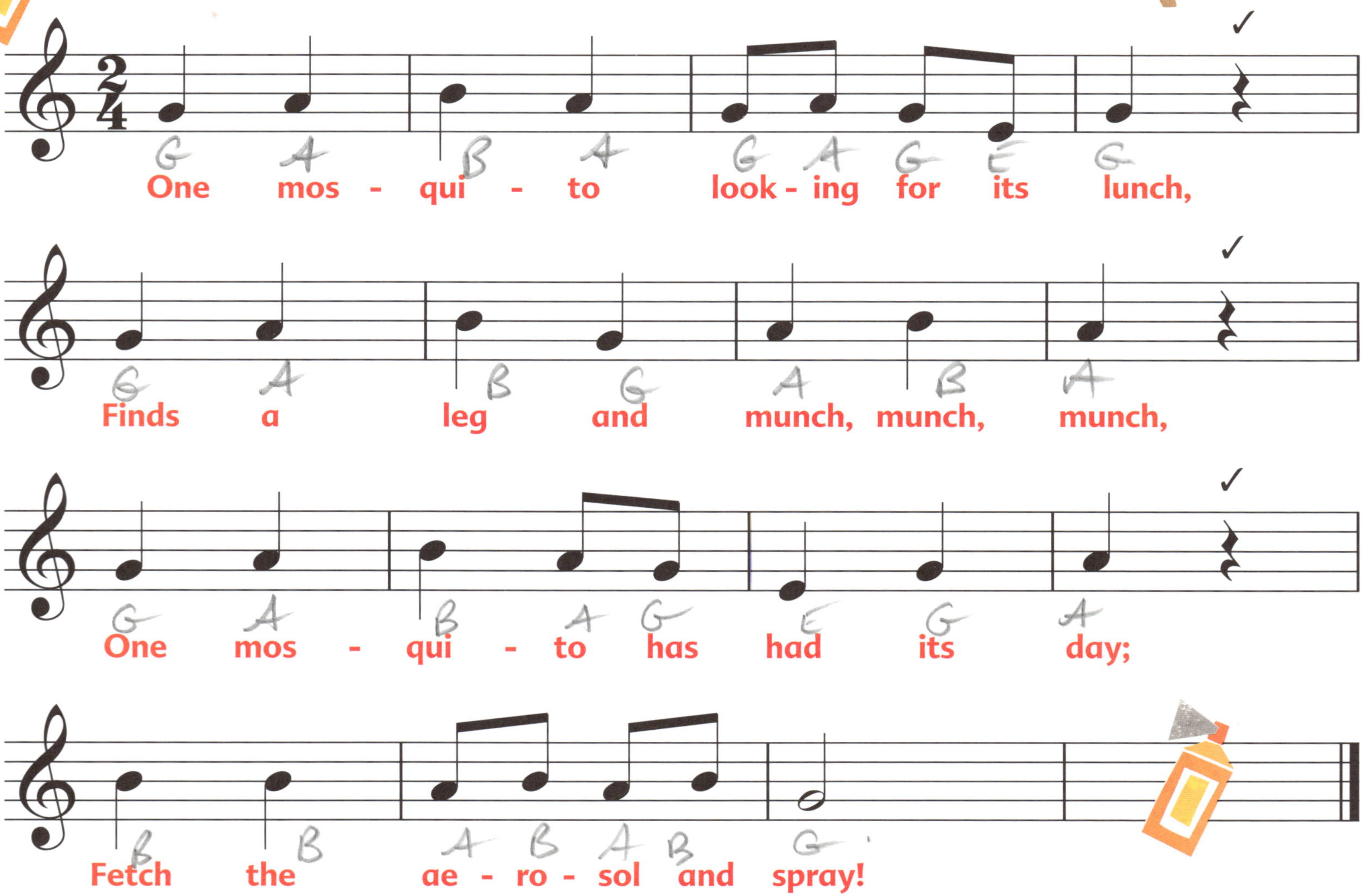

Paint pot

She fell in - to the paint pot,
She fell in - to the sink. Then
she fell in - to the rasp - ber - ry jam and
came out pink, I think!

Tie

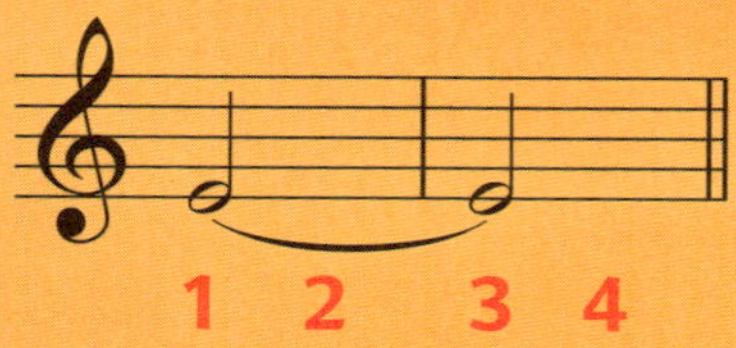

Two notes joined by a tie make one note lasting the length of both notes.
Do not tongue the second note but keep blowing.

Trampolining

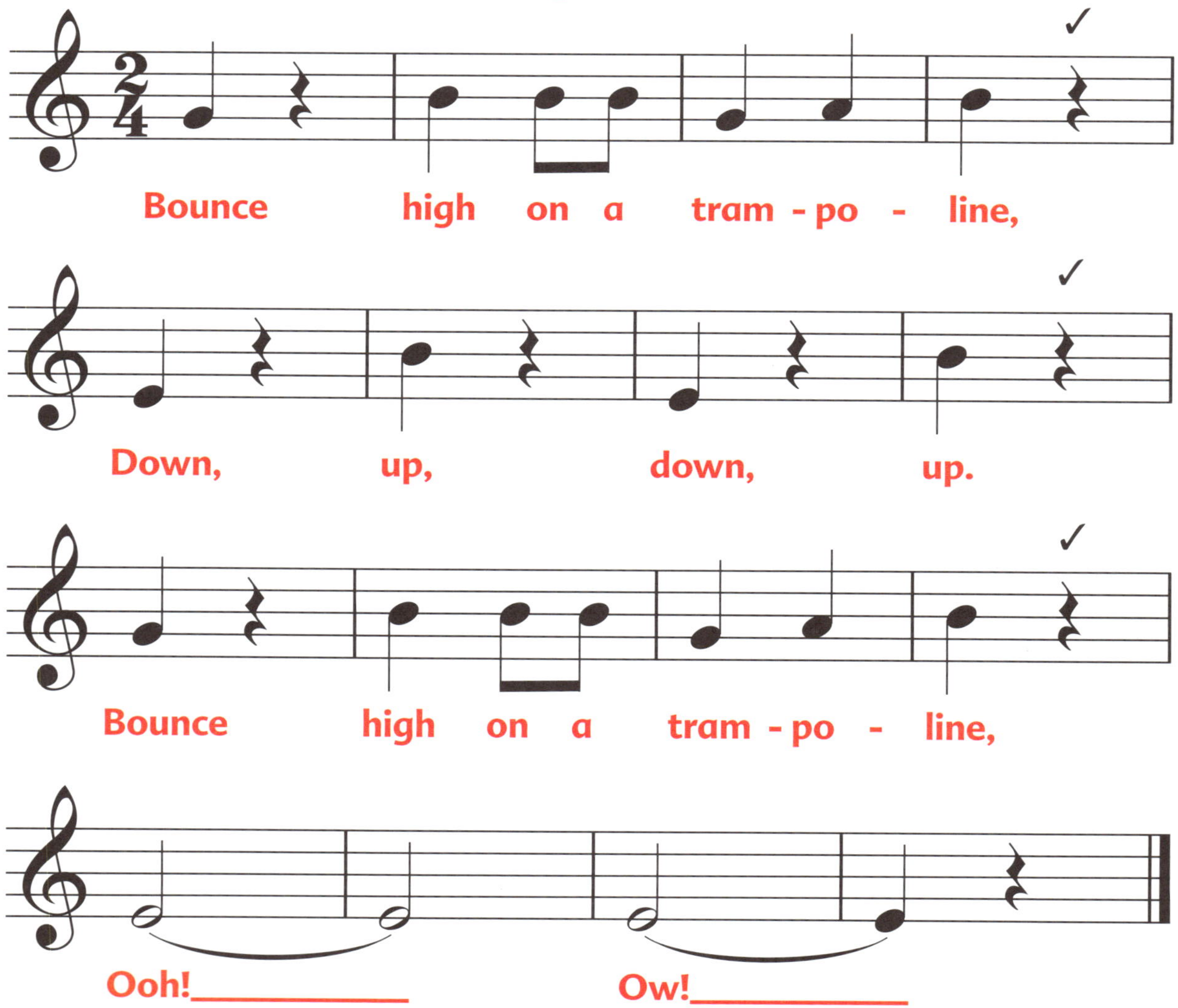

This little bear

New note C

Don't blow - just finger A.
To play C, lift your first finger.

Russian river

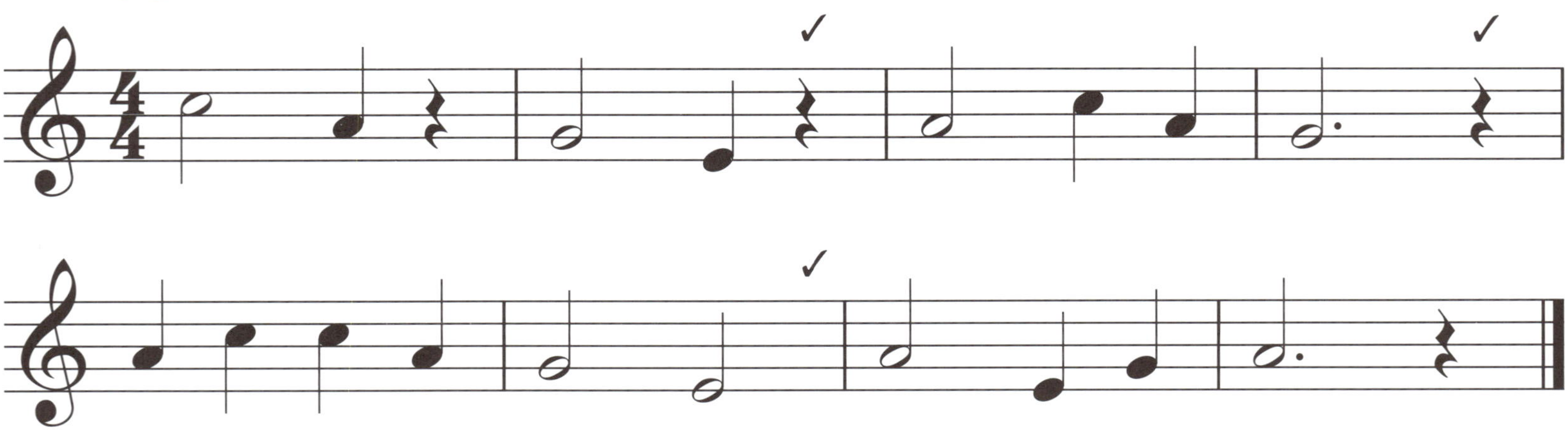

Jog along Jason (duet)

- Play this as a duet. Decide who will play the red and who will play the blue part.
- Swap over for the repeat.
- Then ignore the colours and play the piece all the way through.

Swing high

Pease pudding hot

This can be played as a duet with *Green Jelly* (page 13).

Shepherds' delight

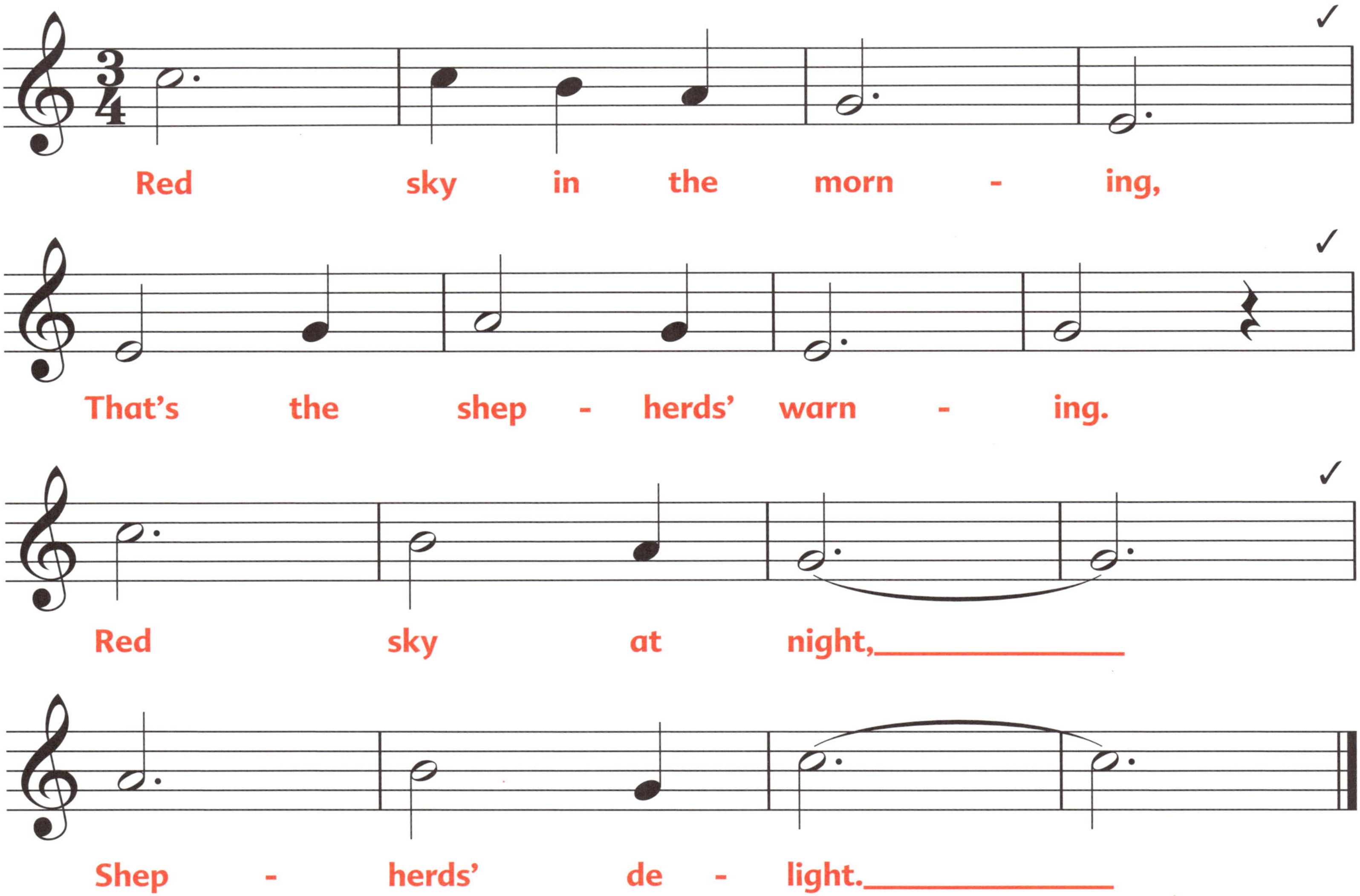

Selfish sharks (round)

Semibreve

o

A semibreve lasts for four beats.

Heave-ho

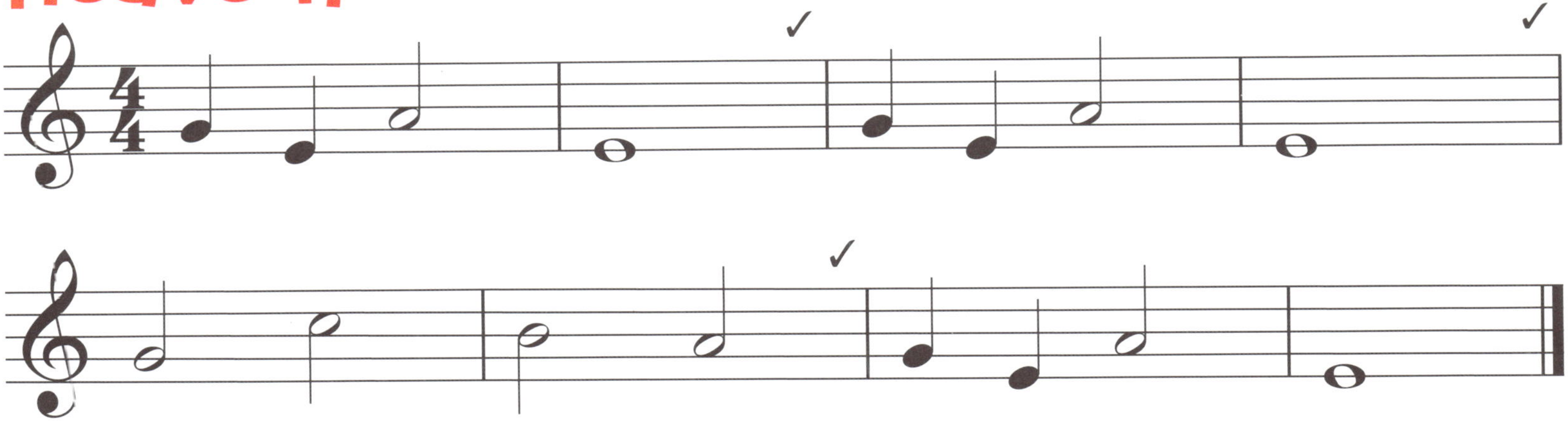

Rigadoon

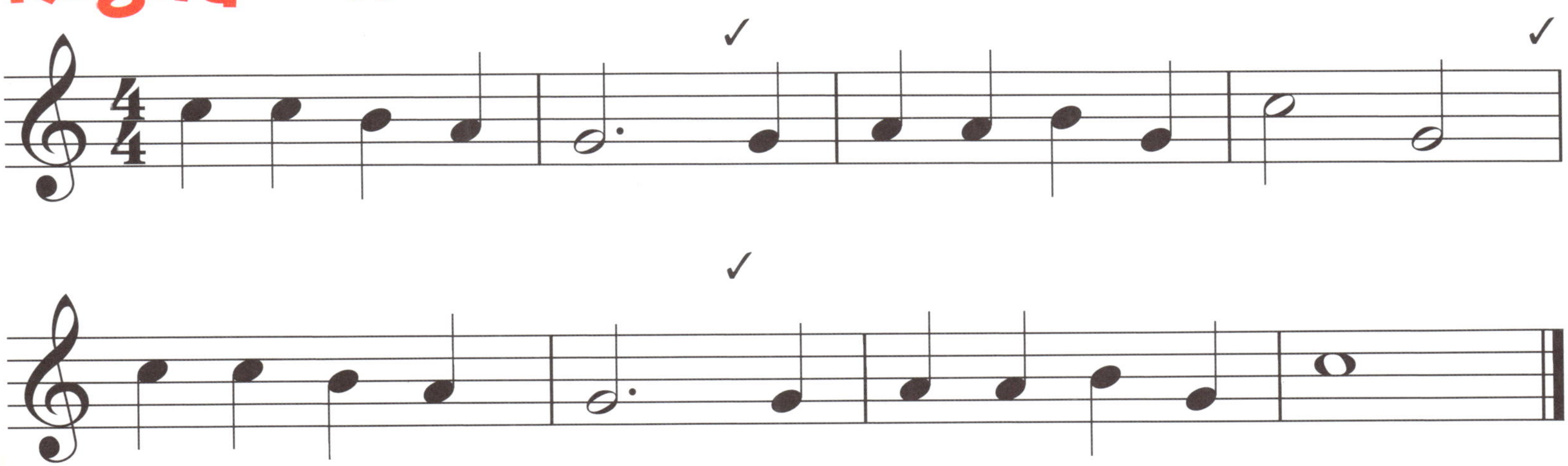

Pigs

Make the squeaks by blowing too hard (overblowing).

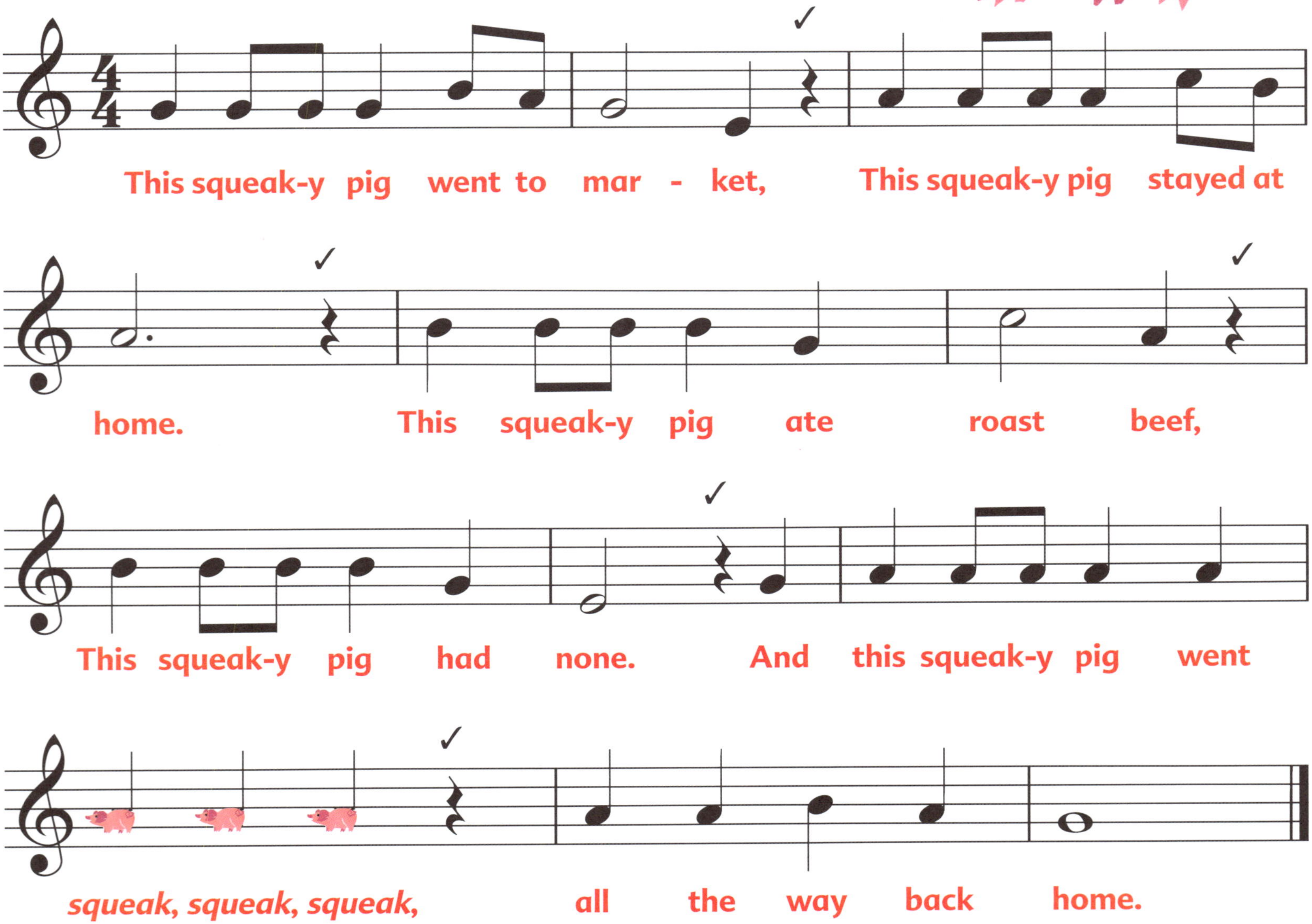

Yes, we have no bananas

Play the tune while someone else performs the claps and shouts.

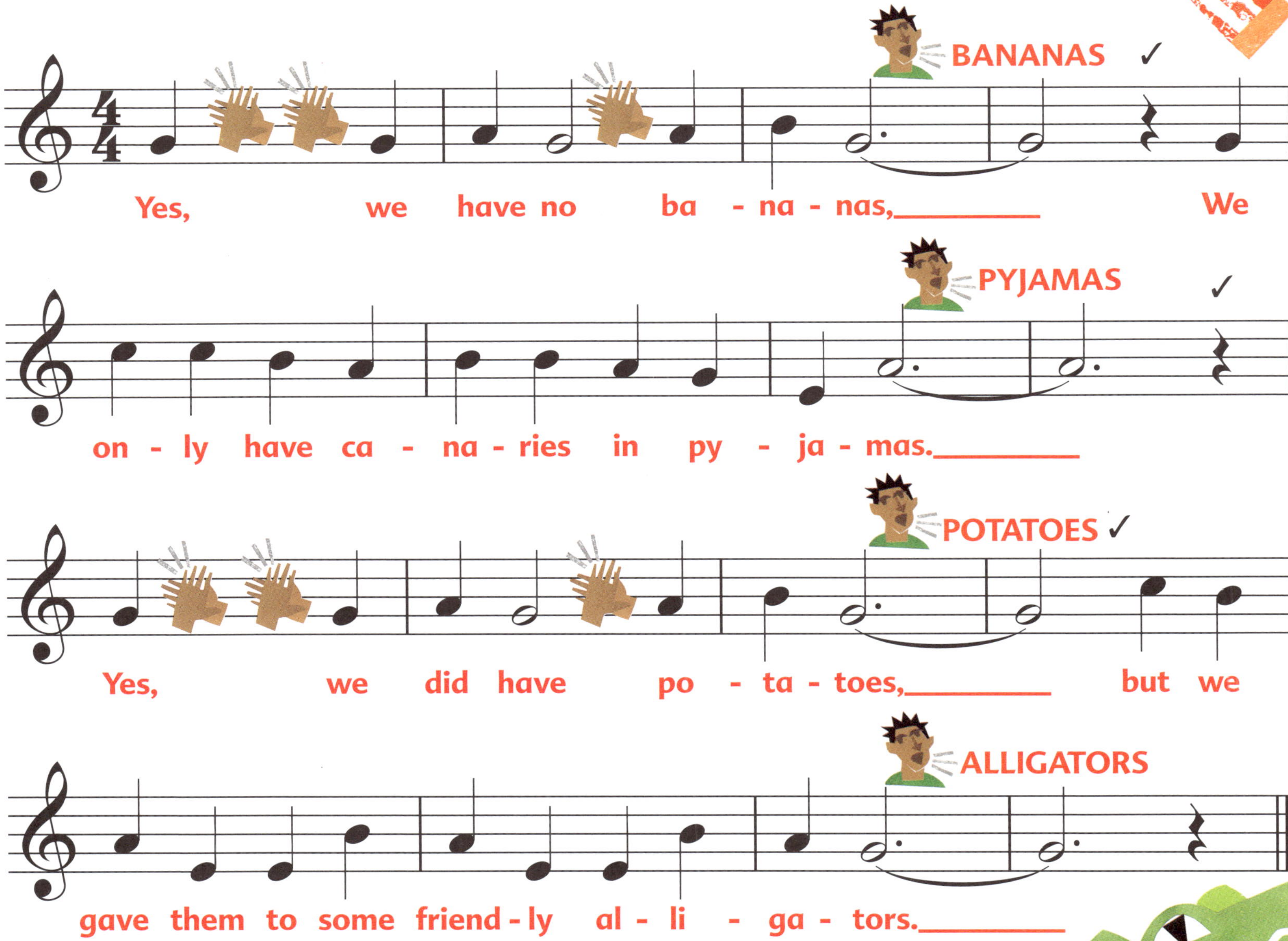

Fingering chart

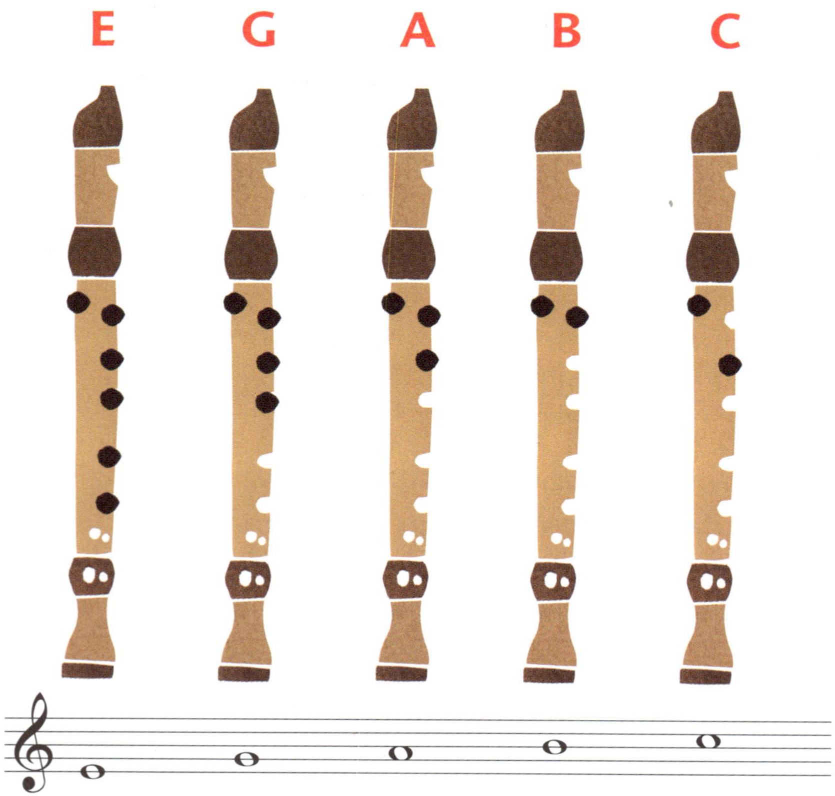

Acknowledgements

The authors and publishers would like to thank all the recorder teachers who assisted in the preparation of this book: Mary Albrighton, Beverley Ann Atherton, Jane Ayles, Sheena Billett, Anne Brooks, Sue Coates, Kate Collings, Mrs S. Dean, Lesley Dolphin, Angela D'Silva, Ann H. Duthie, Anita Felton, Sarah Gardner, Lindsey Giles, Paul Gregory, Avril Grigg, Valerie Henry, Barbara Honeyball, Marta Howard, Chris Jaggard, Carmel Kelly, Sue Klein, Hilary Littlewood, Linda Morse, Judith Mumby, Hilary Oliver, Chris Parrett, Helen Pearce, Catharine Perrin, Ann Sharman, Jeanne Simpson, Anne Snowden, Odette Stephenson, Elaine Sutton, Clare Talbot, Kathleen Thomas, Chris Treggiden, Nicola Walsh and Felicity Ward-Smith.

Special thanks are due to the following consultants: Tom Deveson, Mary Edwards, Linda Evans, Jenny Fisher, Dot Fraser, Grace Gallagher, Maureen Hanke, Derek Kitt, Helen MacGregor, Sue Nicholls, Sheena Roberts, Angela Rodriguez, Liz Stock and Marie Tomlinson.
Thanks also to Tessa Montague for modelling the recorder positions for the illustrator.

First published 2001
by A & C Black (Publishers) Ltd
37 Soho Square, London W1D 3QZ

Reprinted 2001, 2002

Edited by Ana Sanderson and
Emily Haward
Music setting by Emily Haward
Illustrations by Alison Dexter
Designed by Dorothy Moir
Printed in Hong Kong by
Wing King Tong Co Ltd.

ISBN 0 7136 5142 3

www.recordermagic.co.uk